Searched and Known

Searched and Known

An exposition of Psalm 139:1

by

REV. DONALD MACLEAN

REFORMATION PRESS
2018

Published by
Reformation Press, 11 Churchill Drive, Stornoway
Isle of Lewis, Scotland HS1 2NP

www.reformationpress.co.uk

British Library Cataloguing-in-Publication Data
A catalogue record for this book is available from
the British Library

PAPERBACK EDITION
ISBN 978-1-872556-38-3
© Reformation Press 2018

Printed by www.lulu.com

Also available as a Kindle e-book
ISBN 978-1-872556-39-0
© Reformation Press 2018

Contents

Contents

Preface

EVERY so often in our work and our relationships it is worth pausing to take stock and review what we have, how we got here, and what progress we are making. This is also true of our spiritual life. What kind of believer am I? How did I come to know Christ in the first place? Am I growing in my relationship with the Lord and my likeness to Christ? As Donald MacLean points out in this volume, we should be especially careful to take the opportunity to pause and examine ourselves when we consider coming to the end of life, and when we are about to partake of the Lord's Supper.

Over an extended period of time, Mr MacLean delivered a series of sermons on the Book of Psalms at prayer meetings in his congregations in the Free Presbyterian Church of Scotland, firstly in Portree and latterly in Glasgow. He reached Psalm 139 shortly before the administration of the Lord's Supper in the Glasgow congregation. This psalm, with its prominent theme of being scrutinised and searched out by the Lord, provided an opportunity to explore the theme of self-examination in view of the approaching sacrament.

Searched and Known consists of three sermons on Psalm 139:1, 'O Lord, thou hast searched me, and known me'. In the first sermon, Mr MacLean directs his hearers to the treatment of self-examination in the Westminster Larger Catechism, which he uses as the basis of his own remarks. The answer to Larger Catechism question 171 instructs us to prepare ourselves for the Lord's Supper by examining ourselves for evidence of Christian graces and by renewing our exercise of these graces. As is typical of the Larger Catechism, its teaching on this question is detailed, practical, and pastoral. Mr MacLean's sermons pick up on the opening points of the Larger Catechism—we should examine ourselves as to our being in Christ, our sins and needs, and our knowledge, faith and repentance. Although the Larger Catechism goes on to list other areas for self-examination, it appears that the three sermons included in this volume comprise the complete set of Mr MacLean's sermons on this topic on this occasion.

As hearers and readers of Mr MacLean's preaching would expect, these sermons are simultaneously theologically astute and experientially sensitive. His gift for doctrinal clarity is blended once again with his own personal delight in having tasted and felt the redeeming love of the Father, Son and Spirit, and his desire for others to understand and experience God's saving mercy too. As he discusses saving faith and evangelical repentance, he intersperses his remarks with teaching on the nature of Christ's atoning work, various aspects of the meaning of the sacrament, and the difference between faith and assurance, before returning to delineate experiences such as conviction of sin and how the soul embraces and communes with Christ by faith.

These sermons were transcribed verbatim from audio recordings kindly provided by Mr A. J. Morrison, Seilebost, Isle of Harris. The transcripts were then edited to facilitate reading. The guiding principle in editing has been to keep as close as possible to the original wording, while making whatever concessions were necessary for the sake of the reader. These mainly involve small changes to grammar and correction of verbal slips, together with occasional reworking of the text for conciseness or clarity.

A number of conventions have been adopted in this volume. Some of the many Scripture quotations and allusions are referenced in parentheses. Where verses were quoted with minor alterations to fit the context, these have been retained where appropriate rather than giving the exact quotation from the Authorised Version. In quotations from the Scottish Metrical Psalms, line breaks are denoted by a slash mark (/).

The publisher would like to acknowledge with gratitude the help of a number of individuals in the production of this volume. Thanks are due to Flora Campbell for her meticulous transcription. Catherine Hyde assisted with editing and James Dickie designed the cover. The publisher also wishes to record his gratitude to Murdo Mac-Lean, Mr MacLean's younger son, for encouragement to continue publishing his father's sermons and for permission to use a professional photo of his father.

Self-examination is not an end in its own right, of course. It should lead to penitence as we discover more of the sinfulness of our omissions and commissions, a greater sense of our need of Christ to justify and sanctify us, and increased thankfulness to God for the salvation he provides. The publisher would join with Mr MacLean in desiring that these graces would be in exercise and increasing in those who read these sermons, both when they partake of the Lord's Supper from time to time and as they go on through life.

THE PUBLISHER
Stornoway
November 2018

1 Being in Christ

O LORD, thou hast searched me, and known me (Psalm 139:1). This is the keynote to this Psalm. It is very often the case that the psalmist either begins or ends psalms by giving that particular view of divine truth which occupies his mind in that psalm.

Here the psalmist is addressing the Lord and acknowledging him as one who has searched him and known him. Of course, God's searching and God's knowledge is something that he knows all at once. When we search out a matter, such as had to be done in the camp of Israel in the case of Achan, the searching proceeds step by step. But as far as God's searching of us is concerned, he knows us immediately and knows us completely in the way that he alone can know. When he searches us, he takes to do with the thoughts and intents of the heart as well as our outward conduct in this world.

The psalmist's appreciation that God had searched him is bound up with the fact that the psalmist desired that the Lord would continue to search him, or search him again. He says at the end of the psalm, as you remember, 'Search me, O God, and know my heart: try me, and know my thoughts: and see if there be any wicked way in me, and lead me in the way everlasting.' God's guidance in connection with 'the way everlasting', the way of life, the way of everlasting life, is bound up with the Lord searching the soul on the one hand, and on the other hand the soul examining himself or herself in the light of what the Lord gives the soul to know.

Self-examination is a matter that the Lord's people are very much engaged in. Indeed, we should all be engaged in the duty of self-examination, examining ourselves whether we be in the faith. And in order that that may be done we stand in need of the Lord himself searching us and revealing to us his thoughts concerning us in the light of his most holy Word. This is how the soul comes to search himself and to examine himself according to the light that is given to him in his spiritual experience through the Word of God. Therefore we find when the psalmist desired to be led to the hill of God and to the sanctuary of Jehovah and to the altar of God, he prayed, 'Send thy light forth and thy truth; / let them be guides to me' (Psalm 43:3). This is what is needed—this spiritual light, this spiritual illumination, this spiritual knowledge of the Spirit of God—in order that we may examine ourselves in the light of God's truth.

I intend to go through a certain course with this verse, not waiting at the present moment to give a full exposition of it, nor of the verses which follow, but rather dealing with the question of self-examination in the light of God's truth. In view of an approaching communion season it occurred to me that it might be helpful to give consideration to the question of self-examination and the various subjects on which we ought to examine ourselves in the light of divine truth.

Two questions in the Larger Catechism give us valuable guidance on the subject of self-examination.

The first question is: 'How are they that receive the sacrament of the Lord's Supper to prepare themselves before they come unto it?' (Larger Catechism Q 171) The answer is:

> They that receive the sacrament of the Lord's Supper are, before they come, to prepare themselves thereunto, by examining themselves of their being in Christ, of their sins and wants; of the truth and measure of their knowledge, faith, repentance; love to God and the brethren, charity to all men, forgiving those that have done them wrong; of their desires after Christ, and of their new obedience; and by renewing the exercise of these graces, by serious meditation, and fervent prayer.

The subjects covered in this answer are very suitable for someone preparing to commemorate the death of Christ.

The second question, which is very apt to arise as one examines oneself in the light of these various matters is: 'May one who doubteth of his being in Christ, or of his due preparation, come to the Lord's Supper?' (Larger Catechism Q 172). The answer is:

One who doubteth of his being in Christ, or of his due preparation to the sacrament of the Lord's Supper, may have a true interest in Christ, though he be not yet assured thereof; and in God's account hath it, if he be duly affected with the apprehension of the want of it, and unfeignedly desires to be found in Christ, and to depart from iniquity: in which case (because promises are made, and this sacrament is appointed for the relief even of weak and doubting Christians) he is to bewail his unbelief, and labour to have his doubts resolved; and, so doing, he may and ought to come to the Lord's Supper, that he may be further strengthened.

I do not intend to go through all the points mentioned in these answers of the Larger Catechism, but simply to take up a few of the key points.

In examining ourselves on these various points, we must have the assistance of the Lord. We cannot discern the work of grace in our souls unless the Lord enables us to discern it. As we cannot appreciate the work of Christ which he finished on the cross of Calvary unless we are spiritually enlightened, so we cannot understand the work of the Spirit of God in our souls unless we are spiritually enlightened.

Am I in Christ?

On every occasion when we consider commemorating the death of Christ, we must begin by examining ourselves of our being in Christ.

It is only those who are in Christ who can feed upon him, and it is only those who are in Christ who can commemorate his death. And it is only those who are in Christ who can do this in remembrance of him in a proper frame and exercise of soul.

Being 'in Christ' refers to the spiritual union made between Christ and the soul—the spiritual espousal of the soul to Christ and the spiritual union that determines that a soul is in Christ. This union involves two persons: one, the Lord and Saviour Jesus Christ, and the other, a sinner. These two—Christ and the sinner—are united together in a spiritual, a living, a loving and eternal union, in this world. Unless we are united to Christ in this way, we must perish in our sins. As Christ himself said, 'Except ye believe that I am he, ye shall die in your sins' (John 8:24). If we are ever united to him, we know (because the Scripture declares) that neither death, nor life, nor angels, nor principalities, nor powers, nor things present, nor things to come, can separate us from the love of God. Where is that love? It is 'in Christ Jesus our Lord'.

1. Has Christ laid hold of my soul?

Therefore, this question of being in Christ involves first of all Christ's apprehending of the soul by the Holy Spirit. When we examine whether we are a member of Christ's mystical body, or a branch in the true vine, or born again, or regenerated by the Spirit of God, or united to Christ, we must first of all consider Christ laying hold of the soul.

When Christ apprehends the soul by the power of the Holy Spirit, it is done through the Word of God, which liveth and abideth forever. Until Christ lays hold of the soul, it is impossible for the soul to lay hold of Christ, because the soul is by nature dead in trespasses and in sins, and the soul cannot engage in any spiritual activity. It cannot believe, it cannot repent, it cannot love, it cannot die to sin, it cannot forsake sin. It cannot do anything as long as it is in the condition of being spiritually dead. Therefore, the first thing in being 'in Christ' is for Christ by the Holy Spirit to lay hold of the soul, in and by and through the Word of God, to give that soul spiritual life.

When Christ lays hold of the soul, he does so in the exercise of his everlasting love. It is because this soul was loved by the Father and given to the Son, and loved by the Son as the gift of the Father, that the Holy Spirit comes in the fulness of the times, according to the time appointed, to lay hold of the soul. And when the Holy Spirit comes in the name of Christ to lay hold of the soul, the sinner is spiritually quickened, or made spiritually alive. 'You hath he quickened, who were dead in trespasses and sins.' There is no power in this world that can quicken the soul but the power of the Spirit of God. When he quickens the soul, he does so secretly. He does so by a secret exercise of his divine power, down in the depths of the soul.

Now that of course raises the question, 'What does a soul experience when this spiritual quickening takes place?' It is most important for us to notice that in regeneration (or the new birth or effectual calling, whichever name you like to give it) the soul feels the power of the Word of God. The experiences of the soul are bound up with the various effects produced by the Word of God. The Holy Spirit himself cannot be seen. What we see are the effects of his work. 'The wind bloweth where it listeth, but thou canst not tell whence it cometh and whither it goeth.' The Greek word used for Spirit there is 'breath'. That is to say, the breath passes through the leaves of the tree and you wouldn't know it was there unless you saw the movement of the leaves. So, in self-examination what we are concerned with is whether or not we know the effects of the movement of the Holy Spirit in our heart and mind. Just as when we look at a tree and see the leaves moving we know that there is some breath of wind there, so it is with the spiritual experience of the soul. It is by the effects of the Holy Spirit's power exercised in that soul's experience that we come to know what it means to be born again— to be translated out of the kingdom of darkness into the kingdom of God's dear Son and to be brought to the light of the knowledge of the glory of God shining in the person and work of Christ.

These effects are bound up with the Word of God and the doctrines of God's Word. Sometimes the effect comes from particular portions of God's Word, although not necessarily. For some of God's people, certain portions of the Word of God were used to awaken them to a sense of their sins, and certain other portions were used to bring them to the knowledge of Christ, and so on. Others were not dealt with in the same way. The late Mr Macfarlane of Dingwall said that in his experience it wasn't any particular portion of the Word of God but just the Word of God in its entirety that affected him. The important thing is that it's the Word of God, the light of God's Word, the authority of God's truth that the sinner feels. The sinner must feel the Word of God bringing home to him his sins, bringing home his sinnership, bringing home his inability to deliver himself out of the condition in which he finds himself to be, bringing home the fact that he is helpless, unable to deliver himself, certainly unable to satisfy the law of God, certainly unable to satisfy the justice of God, unable also to believe, unable also to repent, unable to do anything that's going to commend him to the mercy of God in any way or to any extent whatsoever. And when Christ brings the soul to this point, this is when he is laying hold on that soul by the Holy Spirit.

2. Have I laid hold of Christ?

As we examine ourselves as to our being in Christ, we must also consider the act of faith on the part of the soul. That is the second point in this union. The Holy Spirit lays hold on the soul in the name of Christ, and the Holy Spirit works in that soul the faith which is of the operation of God. This faith stands not in the wisdom of men, but in the power of God. This faith is altogether supernatural, altogether from the Spirit of God. This faith is wrought in the heart of the sinner in regeneration by the Spirit of God.

But although faith is certainly a grace of the Holy Spirit, it's the sinner who, in exercising that faith, is thus vitally, spiritually, livingly, united to Christ. And we must not think of faith as something that is in one compartment of the soul while love is in another compartment and hope is in another compartment and patience in another. We must be careful to understand that the grace of faith is an exercise of the whole soul.

Faith is also an exercise of a living soul, a soul that has been brought alive by divine power. By divine power the soul has been made conscious of its sinfulness and its inability to deliver itself, and by divine power that soul looks to Christ. That looking to Christ is faith. That soul receives Christ and embraces Christ, and that embracing of Christ is faith. 'As many as received him, to them gave he power to become the sons of God, even to them that believe on his name.'

Again, we must be careful to understand that the Christ who is embraced is the Christ revealed in the Word of God. It is the Christ who is the Son of the Father in truth and love, the Christ who took our nature, the Christ who died for the ungodly, the Christ in whom there is salvation, the Christ who is able to save to the very uttermost, the Christ who loves sinners and who gave himself for them. When the soul discerns Christ in the Word of God—and discerns that the salvation that is in Christ is a salvation altogether suitable to him—then the soul is sweetly drawn by the power of the Spirit of God into union with this glorious one, saying, 'Whom have I in the heavens high / but thee, O Lord, alone? / And in the earth whom I desire / besides thee there is none' (Psalm 73:25). And that exercise of soul, that soul looking to Christ—that's faith! That soul's dependence on Christ—that's faith!

3. The difference between faith and assurance

Now this brings me to mention one point that has brought a great deal of confusion to many genuine souls because of the loose way in which it is sometimes spoken of—that is, the difference between faith and assurance.

Christ is the object of faith. Christ is presented in the everlasting gospel as the one who died and who rose again and whose blood is able to cleanse from all sin. Christ is the one in whom there is eternal salvation. God says that whosoever believeth in Christ shall not perish but have everlasting life. Faith unites the soul to Christ as the Saviour of sinners. The soul realises, 'I am a sinner, an empty sinner, a vile sinner, an undone sinner, a sinner who cannot deliver myself,' and now in the exercise of faith, the soul says, 'Christ has been made precious to my soul by the Holy Spirit, and I embrace him, I believe in him, I trust in him, I embrace him.' That's faith, as distinct from assurance.

Now the gospel does not call a sinner to believe that Christ died for him. That's very important. If you were called to believe that Christ died for you, that would mean that you were called to believe you are saved, which is in

20

fact assurance and not faith. But a sinner who is exercising faith for the first time is exercising faith *in order* to be saved, not because they know they are saved. Certainly the apostle spoke of 'the Son of God, who loved me and, gave himself for me'. But that's not faith, that's assurance! What we're talking about just now is the first exercise of faith that unites the soul to the divine Redeemer. The sinner exercises faith in Christ as the Saviour of sinners, as distinct from having assurance that Christ is the one who died for me. As Paul says, 'This is a faithful saying, and worthy of all acceptation, that Christ Jesus came into the world to save sinners.' That's the presentation of Christ in the everlasting gospel which faith has to do with.

Arminians, and others who are in effect Arminians although they go under the name of Calvinists, tell sinners that what they've got to do is to believe that Christ died for them, and if they believe that Christ died for them, then they'll be saved. But how? How can I believe that Christ died for me if I don't know that I'm among the elect? How can I believe that Christ died for me without looking into the Lamb's book of life and finding my name written there? And it's not possible to do that. Therefore, the Christ I must look to is the Christ who died for sinners. The Christ I look to is the Christ of whom the Father said, 'Whosoever believeth in him shall not perish, but have everlasting life.'

Therefore, in the first exercise of faith I believe in Christ for the salvation of my soul. And *then*—united to him and under the shelter of his blood—*then* I can rejoice in the fact that Christ died for me, that he rose again for me, that he is in heaven at God's right hand for me. But in the first exercise of faith, what the gospel is concerned with is presenting a Saviour who died for the ungodly, who died for sinners. Faith embraces Christ in that light. Faith says, in effect, 'I embrace Christ for the salvation of my soul. I embrace Christ for the pardon of my sins. I look to Christ for salvation.' That's faith!

This then is the second strand in the soul's union to Christ. There is both Christ's laying hold of the soul and the soul's laying hold of Christ. Laying hold of Christ cannot be done by any soul apart from the power of the Spirit of God. It cannot be done in truth and reality by any sinner apart from divine power. When the soul, in this frame— as a guilty, lost, empty, helpless, hell-deserving sinner— looks by faith to Christ as the Saviour of the lost and the undone, then he's in Christ from that very moment. He is in Christ, whether he can discern it or not. If there is this disposition in the soul—if the soul is turning away from all that pertains to himself and looking to Christ for salvation—then that soul is in Christ, united to Christ for time and for eternity. He is united to Christ because the Holy Spirit in the name of Christ laid hold of him, and because the Holy Spirit in the name of Christ quickened him and wrought in him this faith that looks to Christ alone for salvation.

Am I conscious of sins and needs?

Now just a word on the need for those who are to receive the Lord's Supper to examine themselves as to their sins and wants.

Next to our being in Christ, the Larger Catechism refers to examining ourselves as to our sins and wants. These two things are not incompatible. For a sinner to be in Christ, for a sinner to be a new creature, for a sinner to be united to Christ by faith, does not mean that he no longer has sins and it does not mean that he no longer has wants.

Those who are in Christ, their sins are pardoned. Those who are in Christ, their sins are forgiven. But the very fact that they're in Christ makes sin exceeding sinful to them. The very fact that they're in Christ makes their sins a burden to them. The very fact that they're in Christ makes their backslidings of heart a pain and a sorrow to them.

Yet those who are in Christ, their wants and needs are all supplied. Again, this very fact makes them feel poor in spirit. But as the Scripture says, 'Blessed are the poor in spirit: for theirs is the kingdom of heaven.' Theirs is the kingdom of God, and theirs is the King of the kingdom, and theirs are the storehouses of the kingdom, and theirs is the fulness that is in the kingdom. That fulness is there for those who say, 'I poor and needy am, yet of me the Lord a care will take' (Psalm 40:17).

Their fulness is in their divine head, their fulness is in the storehouses of the Joseph of the New Testament. That is where the fulness lies. Riches, unsearchable riches, are in Christ, and the heirs of this world, the heirs of promise, live on these riches. And as they live on these riches they themselves are poor in themselves. Although their language is, 'I poor and needy am,' yet Christ says with regard to them, 'Blessed are the poor in spirit: for theirs is the kingdom of heaven,' and so on. They say of themselves what Paul says of himself, 'O wretched man that I am! Who shall deliver me from the body of this death?' They are conscious that they are sinners still, although they are sinners saved by grace, sinners who are looking to the fulness that is in Christ to deliver them eventually from all their sins and their iniquities.

Therefore, in their self-examination about their being in Christ, they are not to take the fact that they have sins and the fact that they have wants and to conclude that these disprove the fact that they are in Christ. It is the experience of God's people, that a 'disease that loathsome is / so fills their loins with pain, / that in their weak and weary flesh / no soundness doth remain' (Psalm 38:7). They are poor and needy in their spiritual experience in this world, dependent upon the fulness that is in Christ.

In these sins and wants, in the consciousness that they have of coming short with every breath they draw, the consciousness that they have of wants that are many—their wants of holiness, their wants of thirst, their wants of hunger in a spiritual sense, their blindness, their deadness, their coldness, their barrenness, all that gives them grief and sorrow in this world—in the midst of all this, their disposition and the inclination and exercise of their heart and mind is to look to Christ. It is that disposition of which we read in Psalm 34: 'They looked to him, and lightened were: / not shamed were their faces. / This poor man cried'—this man who had been enlightened, this man who was never to be put to shame—'This poor man cried, God heard, and saved / him from all his distresses.'

This is true in connection with them, that whatever sins and whatever wants they may have, they know where there is a fulness to cleanse them, a fulness to satisfy them, a fulness to give them to say, 'As with marrow and with fat / my soul shall filled be' (Psalm 63:5). They know where that fulness is, and that fulness is in Christ, and therefore they look to him and they cry to him and they wait on him with expectation.

May he bless his Word.

2 Knowledge and faith

THE duty of self-examination is one that is impressed upon every one of us. We are to examine ourselves whether we be in the faith—whether Jesus Christ is in us, and whether we are ourselves in him. In order that we may conduct such self-examination in a way that would be profitable to us and to God's glory, we must have both David's acknowledgement and David's prayer. He acknowledged, 'O Lord, thou hast searched me, and known me,' and then as we read later on in the Psalm, he prayed, 'Search me, O God, and know my heart.'

God's searching and knowing of us is altogether different from our searching and knowing of ourselves. God searches us and knows us in one act of his infinite mind. By one glance of his infinite and eternal mind he knows us through and through. It is not necessary for him to conduct any searching into us that would reveal something he did not know already. The Lord's knowledge of us is something that he knows immediately and (as theologians say) intuitively. But when we search ourselves, it must be a process by which we move from step to step. Consequently, we are continually dependent on the light of

God's Word and on the instruction and drawing and leading of God the Holy Spirit to do this duty.

Self-examination and the Lord's Supper

The duty of self-examination is particularly required of those who intend to commemorate the death of Christ. The Scripture says, 'Let a man examine himself, and so let him eat of this bread and drink of this cup' (1 Corinthians 11:28). Here those who partake of the Lord's Supper are called to examine themselves. They are called to prepare themselves by their self-examination for a proper, God-glorifying, soul-sanctifying commemoration of the death of Christ.

Such activity does not pertain merely to the first time that a person comes to the Lord's Table. Undoubtedly, on the first occasion, a person's self-examination is often attended by considerable concern of mind. Part of that concern undoubtedly arises from spiritual ignorance on that person's part, his or her inability to come to come to conclusions with regard to their spiritual experiences, whether they are saving or whether they are not saving.

But however long we have been commemorating the death of Christ, surely it should be true on every occasion that we sit at the Lord's Table that we will be concerned to be in a proper frame of soul. We are called to commemorate the Lord's death often, as we read, 'As often as ye eat this bread and drink this cup, ye do show the Lord's death till he come' (1 Corinthians 11:26). But we must be careful that, in seeking to obey that injunction, we do not become careless, that we do not become formalists, and that we do not lose sight of the value and the preciousness of the ordinance of the Lord's Supper. One of the ways to prevent us from becoming careless is for us to ever have before our mind the duty of self-examination, the duty of preparing ourselves for such an occasion.

Self-examination regarding death and judgment

Self-examination is also required with regard to having a proper frame of mind in view of death and judgment. There are many people nowadays who profess religion and who have great assurance. They seem to think that it's part of their faith that they should have such great assurance, to the extent that they seem to have lost any proper concern for the reality of their soul's saving interest in Christ. That is a very bad sign, a sign that their assurance is not of a very healthy nature.

Let me illustrate this particular point in this way. If I take a train journey from Glasgow to London I must buy a ticket at the Central Station to go down to Euston in London. I pay my fare, I receive my ticket. Now once I am some way down the line, I might put my hand in my pocket to make sure the ticket is still there. That's a proper concern. I want to be sure that I will arrive with my ticket and so be able to pass through the barrier when I come to Euston. If I did not concern myself about my ticket and I lost it on the way, when I came to the barrier at Euston, I would not be able pass through without going through an endless rigmarole in order to establish the fact that I had indeed received a ticket at the Central Station.

Translated to the spiritual sphere, there is a proper concern which leads to self-examination. When I come to death and judgment, I want to be sure that I will not be found wanting. There is little doubt that for many, towards the end of their days, when they're coming towards the barrier of death and about to enter into eternity, much of the concern and trouble they have in connection with their soul arises from their failure to examine themselves as they ought to have done while they were on the way in this world.

Therefore we can see the necessity of self-examination from these two points of view, both with regard to death and judgment and also in particular on these occasions of commemorating the death of Christ.

Preparation for the Lord's Supper

You remember that I promised to give an explanation of the question in the Larger Catechism, 'How are they that receive the sacrament of the Lord's Supper to prepare themselves before they come unto it?' As I have been saying already, they are to prepare themselves by examining themselves 'of their being in Christ' and 'of their sins and wants'.

Now, we are also told in the Larger Catechism that those who sit at the Lord's Table are to examine themselves on 'the truth and measure of their knowledge, faith and repentance'. They are to examine themselves on two things in connection with these graces of the Spirit. First of all, they are to examine themselves of the *truth* of them—that is to say, of the reality of them—whether they really and truly have them. Further, they are to examine themselves on the *measure* of them—what degree of them they possess. In other words, they are first to examine themselves as to the root—the possession of these graces— and then they are also to examine themselves as to the fruit—the actual measure of knowledge, the actual measure of faith, the actual measure of repentance, the actual measure of love to God and the brethren, and so on. They are not to be content merely with discovering that they have these graces, but they are also to examine themselves as to the measure of them.

1. Do I have real knowledge?

The first thing that is brought before us here is their knowledge. They are to examine themselves as to the reality of their knowledge. This includes their knowledge of God, their knowledge of the things of the Spirit of God, their knowledge of Christ, their knowledge of union to Christ, their knowledge of spiritual things.

Of course, this does not mean that they are to examine themselves just on their knowledge of the Bible, the history of the Bible, the events that took place in the Bible, or even the doctrines of the Bible. That knowledge is necessary. It's undoubtedly necessary for making a true profession of faith. They are also to examine themselves as to their knowledge of the things of the Spirit of God in particular. That's what the Scripture says. The Scripture does not say that the natural man understandeth not the doctrines of God's Word. He may do so. He may be able to repeat the Shorter Catechism. He may be able to listen to a sermon and find fault if he finds doctrinal error. The natural man can do these things, but what the Scripture says is that the natural man understandeth not the things of the Spirit of God. 'Eye hath not seen, nor ear heard, neither have entered into the heart of man, the things which God hath prepared for them that love him, but God hath revealed them unto us by his Spirit (1 Corinthians 2:9–10). There is a passing through the veil of doctrine and passing into a soul knowledge and a soul communion and a soul relish and a soul delight in the things that God hath prepared for those that love him. This is of course a vast subject which could take up many sermons. But I'll confine myself on the present occasion just to making one or two remarks on spiritual knowledge.

This knowledge includes knowledge of God. You find the Saviour saying, 'This is life eternal, that they might know thee, the only true God, and Jesus Christ, whom thou hast sent.' We were singing in the Psalm (89:15), 'O greatly blessed the people are / the joyful sound that know.' That's spiritual knowledge. The knowledge that is bound up with eternal life is spiritual knowledge.

This knowledge springs from the operation of the Spirit of God in the heart of a sinner. It's quite true that it is a good thing for people to have doctrine explained to them. That is the function of the ministry, which is why minsters are to be apt to teach (1 Timothy 3:2)—they are to be teachers in the things of the Spirit of God. But the fact still remains that however clearly the doctrines of God's Word may be taught, however clearly the things of the Spirit of God may be opened up in the preaching of the gospel, and however repeatedly they may be explained, a sinner will never grasp or understand those spiritual realities apart from the Holy Spirit operating in his soul. Paul tells us, 'God, who commanded the light to shine out of darkness, hath shined in our hearts to give us the light of the knowledge of the glory of God in the face of Jesus Christ' (2 Corinthians 4:6). It's spiritual knowledge—the light of the knowledge of the glory of God—and it's given by the Holy Spirit in the heart. It doesn't merely come into the heart out of the Word, but it's *in* the heart, so that when the sinner hears the Word of God and reads the Word of God and meditates on the Word of God, the Holy Spirit is shining in his soul, giving him to receive and embrace and rest on the things revealed in the Word of God.

Now let me come down more particularly to what we are directly concerned about just now. The knowledge especially required in connection with commemorating the death of Christ is knowledge to discern the Lord's body.

The first thing that I would remark on with reference to discerning the Lord's body is that it includes in the sinner's mind and soul and conscience a distinct difference between the table of the Lord and every other table in this world. That's very important. In the Corinthian church, they were eating and drinking as if the Lord's Supper was any ordinary meal. They were even drunk at the Lord's Supper (1 Corinthians 11:21). They were treating it as a common meal, in the backslidden condition that they were in. They had this defect in their knowledge, that they did not understand that the Lord's Table was distinct from every other table, distinct from the table of devils of course, and distinct from the table in their own homes.

The Lord's Table has the elements of the broken body and the shed blood of Christ, it has Christ as its glorious head, it is a table concerning which he says, 'Eat and drink! Eat, O friends; drink, yea drink abundantly, O beloved.' The soul who discerns the Lord's body knows, even without any fencing of the table, that there is a distinction between this table and every other table in this world. If you have that knowledge in your heart and in your experience and in your conscience, you make a distinction between the Lord's Table and every other table in the world, and between this communion and every other communion in the world. The table in your own home, however precious it may be to you, is something altogether different, altogether distinct. The Lord's Table is something that pertains to the kingdom of God, a kingdom which is spiritual, and which involves spiritual knowledge and spiritual communion and fellowship.

The second thing in this spiritual knowledge is the knowledge of the Lord's body as set before us in the signs of the Lord's Table.

Let us note in passing that the administration of the Lord's Supper is a ministerial act—not the act of a kirk session. The kirk session examines those who come forward and they exercise the power of the keys by opening and closing the door to this ordinance, but the actual administration of the sacrament is a ministerial act. The elders are there to carry round the bread and wine, but the kirk session is not involved in the act of dispensing the Lord's Supper. As the Westminster Confession of Faith says (chapter 29, paragraph 3), the sacrament is only to be dispensed by a minister of the Word, lawfully ordained. The minister, in Christ's name, using the words of institution (1 Corinthians 11:24–25) says, 'Take, eat: this is my body, which is broken for you,' and, 'This cup is the new testament in my blood.'

Well, the knowledge to discern the Lord's body which is required at the Lord's Table is bound up with the knowledge of what the bread and the wine mean. It is bound up with the knowledge that without the shedding of blood there is no remission. The soul looks beyond the bread and the wine and lays hold by faith of what the bread and the wine symbolise, namely that without the shedding of blood there is no remission of sin.

Now a sinner may know it doctrinally and he may agree with it, because it's in the Word of God and he cannot disagree that without the shedding of blood there is no remission of sin. But there is such a thing as having spiritual knowledge of that—of being brought to realise what sin is, of being brought to realise what sin deserves, that sin deserves death, of being brought to realise that my sins deserve death, and that if God was to deal with me according to my sins, then death would be my portion for time and for eternity. There is that in it.

And there is this too in this knowledge, the consciousness that nothing short of the blood of the Lamb of God could atone for my sins, that nothing short of the death that was accomplished outside the gates of Jerusalem could atone for one sin of mine, let alone the multitude of them. Nothing short of the death of the Son of God and his drinking the cup that the Father gave him to drink could possibly atone for my sins and my iniquities and my transgressions. All of that is bound up with the pardon of sin.

Therefore, in this knowledge, there is a spiritual knowledge of sin, its deserts, its evil. The sinner is willing to acknowledge, 'I have sinned with my fathers and I am no more worthy of the least of all thy mercies.'

On the other hand, there is a spiritual knowledge of Christ and the sacrifice of Christ. There is a soul appreciation and a soul understanding of what it cost the divine Redeemer to pay the ransom price he paid for the remission of the sins of many. There is an understanding of what Christ said with regard to this point, 'My flesh is meat indeed, and my blood is drink indeed.'

So, if we have any reality to our knowledge, this means that I am conscious of what my sins and my iniquities deserve, that they deserve death, and I am conscious that nothing short of the blood of the everlasting covenant, nothing short of the blood of the Lamb of God, nothing short of the sufferings unto death of the Lord of glory, could have been sufficient to atone for my sins. I see and I understand all this, and I receive him as all my salvation and all my desire. I believe that there is no other name given under heaven among men whereby I can be saved but Christ alone. This is the reality of spiritual knowledge.

2. What is the measure of my knowledge?

Those who receive the Lord's Supper are also to examine themselves as to the measure of their spiritual knowledge. Now the reality may be very small, in the sense that it has still to grow. Of course, it is not small in the sense that it is the work of the Holy Spirit and none but the Spirit of God can give it. But even when the knowledge is very small, it is knowledge that is sufficient to bring the soul to the feet of Christ. It is knowledge that is sufficient to give the soul to understand and to believe and to rest upon Christ alone for salvation. It is knowledge that is sufficient to make the sinner cast away every rag of his own right-eousness, and to rest in Christ and to rest in him alone for salvation. That's the reality of it.

But regarding the measure of it, they are to examine themselves as to how they are growing in this knowledge. For example, how are they getting fresh light on the awfulness of sin and the evil of sin? There are some people who don't like sermons about sin, say, on the Sabbath morning of a communion. I've heard of such complaints being made. What they want to hear about on the Sabbath of a communion is about the love of Christ and so on. That's what they say, and they don't want to hear about sin and death in the sermon before the Lord's Supper. Well, I don't understand that kind of religion, because I don't see how sinners can ever come to properly appreciate the love of Christ unless they understand the evil of sin—unless they understand what the Saviour meant when he said, 'Reproach hath broke my heart; I'm full / of grief: I looked for one / to pity me, but none I found; / comforters found I none' (Psalm 69:20). What made him say that? The fact that he was bearing the reproach of his people's sin. If people do not understand the evil of sin and the bitterness of sin and the awfulness of sin, they'll never come to understand the love of Christ.

We should be growing in a soul abhorrence of sin, and a soul abhorrence of our own sin. When we come to handle with the hand of our bodies the symbol of the broken body of Christ, and handle with the mouth of our bodies the wine that represents the poured-out blood of the Son of God, surely, my dear friend, we should do so as sinners. I have often spoken of that poor woman, who had such a sense of her sinnership that, when the wine was handed to her, she shrank from taking it. But Dr Duncan said to her, 'Tak' it, woman, it's for sinners.' Dr Duncan had this knowledge himself—he knew he was a sinner—he knew that the love of Christ was for sinners.

Let us also consider the measure of our growing in the knowledge of Christ—Christ's person, Christ's work, Christ's fulness, Christ's death and Christ's love. We must examine our growing in the knowledge of these things, our getting fresh light on them, our hearts being attracted by them, our souls being drawn to them, our souls delighting in them. Some of the older people here will remember a man in Ness called Malcolm Macleod. He was a missionary there for many a day. One of the things he used to say in speaking to the question was this: 'Where did love go when it left the affections?' Perhaps it's not very exact theologically, but it's a good experimental explanation of the matter. The Christian had warm affections at the beginning, and they lived on these affections and they thought they could not commemorate the death of Christ without these affections. But after a time in the Christian life, the affections may cease to be so lively. So Malcolm Macleod asked, 'Where did love go when it left the affections?' He said, 'It went to the understanding.' You see, this is the great thing. Where there is growth in spiritual knowledge, this will have its own fruit in the sanctifying of the affections—not necessarily the movement of the mere emotions, but the sanctifying of the affections—so that the soul delights himself in God and rejoices in God's salvation. After all, this is what the Lord's Supper is for, that God's people may rejoice.

3. Do I have real faith?

Those who receive the Lord's Supper are also to examine themselves as to the truth and measure of their faith. Faith, where it is in reality, goes out to Christ in the everlasting gospel. Christ is the object of justifying faith, and the soul goes out to Christ in the exercise of faith, in dependence on his fulness, in dependence on the merit of his blood, in dependence on his grace, in dependence on his compassion. 'Lord, pity me' is the call of this soul.

They are also to examine the reality of their faith in connection with the Word of God. You see, although faith in its first exercise—justifying faith, as we call it, to distinguish it from other kinds of faith—goes towards Christ, yet it takes in the whole of the Word of God. Faith that has reality is bound up with a soul appreciation of the Word of God, and a soul appreciation of the light of God's Word, a soul appreciation of living a life of dependence on the Word of God.

And then we are to examine ourselves of the measure of our faith—whether it is faith to feed on Christ. The faith that feeds on Christ is the open mouth of the soul desiring to receive Christ. That is what faith is doing, in coming to the Lord's Table. 'Open thy mouth wide,' the Scripture says, 'and I will fill it abundantly.' When a soul comes to the Lord's Table, what Christ says through his ministering servant at this table is, 'Take, eat! Take, eat!' That's what Christ is going to say. 'This is my body broken for you. This cup is the new testament in my blood. Drink ye all of it!' So what is required of the soul at that time is the open mouth of faith. Christ encourages the soul to say, 'I'll of salvation take the cup, / on God's name will I call' (Psalm 116:13). When faith comes to the Lord's Table it's coming for something—it's coming for feeding, and it's coming for refreshing and its coming for strengthening and it's coming for nourishment.

Now I put it to you, is it not very often the case for many in coming to the Lord's Table, that they won't come unless they've already been nourished, they won't come unless they've already been strengthened, they won't come unless they've already been encouraged? This is the kind of exercise that they have, 'If I would I get something for my soul, *then* how easy it would be for me to go to the Lord's Table!' Well, so it might be, but then I doubt very much if you'll get anything at the Table itself. When a person invites you to come to his house because he is going to spread a table before you, you don't say, 'Well, if he would send some of it through the post so I would get some of it before I arrived, then I would be encouraged to go.' You wouldn't do that in a natural way, and yet, you see, because of spiritual darkness, we're very much inclined to want to do that in the spiritual way. Of course, I'm speaking just now about the sinner that's been born again. Of course, a sinner must have the new birth before he comes to the Lord's Table. Obviously. He can't have hunger and he can't have thirst before he does. But where you have one of the Lord's people, someone who is truly born again, then to him or her this commandment,

'This do in remembrance of me', has become a weight and a burden that they cannot escape from and cannot cast off, and yet they hesitate to come because they fear their faith is not strong enough.

But in being encouraged to come to the Lord's Table, they are to come to be fed, they're to come to be nourished. What we call the action sermon—that is, the sermon before the action of the breaking of the bread and the pouring out of the wine—is all intended to help and encourage the person to commemorate the death of Christ for their nourishment. It's to bring before them these great truths on which the soul is to be fed in his or her spiritual experience. The same thing is true with regard to the addresses which are given at the Lord's Table by ministers of the gospel. The purpose of the table address is to help—that's all it is—to help the Lord's people to meditate on what they ought to meditate on—on Christ, his death, his love, his offices, his person, his work, and all the fulness that is in him—so that they might be fed.

The communicant in coming to the Lord's Table is coming to be fed, he's coming to be nourished, he's coming to be strengthened, he's coming empty in himself, looking to the Lord to bless him, to meet with him, to manifest himself to him, and to feed him spiritually in his heart and mind. I must emphasise that the Lord's Table is for the nourishment of God's people. That should never be forgotten. That's the reason why Christ instituted it in the Church of God. It's not an occasion for Satan to make trouble—that's his work, that proceeds from him, and of

41

course he'll be busily engaged in it—but it's for feeding God's people. When a person is examining himself or herself and perhaps finding themselves without the comforts and consolations that they would like to have, they're to come for these blessings. They've received them already in their first coming to Christ and they've been growing in the experience of them to some extent. However great or however small the measure may be, their prayer is, 'Lord, increase our faith,' that they might grow in grace and in the knowledge of the Lord and Saviour Jesus Christ.

As they are engaged in this, and as this Table is spread for them in the church, in the wilderness of this world, Christ is saying to them, 'Take, eat: this is my body broken for you,' and, 'This cup is the new testament in my blood.' He also says, 'As often as ye eat this bread, and drink this cup, ye do show the Lord's death till he come.' That's the witnessing part, but the primary part is the feeding. The primary part is the refreshing, the primary part is for the soul to partake of that which is spiritually represented by the bread and the wine, the 'wine that maketh glad the heart of man'. There's nothing, my dear friend, that will gladden the heart of the child of God compared to feeding on Christ in the communion of God's people at a communion table. This is the gallery of the king in an outstanding way.

If we were more concerned with casting the eye of our soul to Christ in coming to the Lord's Table, then we wouldn't bother so much with others, or with the world, or with Satan. The way to get rid of them is to have our eye to Christ and to the words of Christ, 'Take, eat: this is my body which is broken for you.' If we would focus on Christ, we would find faith in living exercise at the Lord's Table far more than we ordinarily find it to be.

This is something that we need to pray over. In coming to the Lord's Table, what are we really coming for? Do we know? Do we understand? Christ tells us what he has for us: 'This is my body, and this cup is the new testament in my blood.' There's spiritual nourishment, there's spiritual strengthening, there's spiritual refreshment at the Lord's Table. Christ is there. We are called to believe that Christ is there, and we are called to hope that we would get a crumb from the master's table and be enabled to drink out of the cup of salvation. Our eye is to be to the divine Redeemer and to his purpose in the institution of the Supper, which is to feed his people, to strengthen them, to manifest to them that he delights in them as a people near to him. They may smite upon their breast and complain about how dark, how brutish, how cold and how dead they are in their approaches to these holy and spiritual things, even to the extent that they are sometimes tempted to turn back. But there is something in faith, my dear friend, that still turns to Christ, and there's something in faith that still says, 'So henceforth we will not go back, / nor turn from thee at all: / O do thou quicken us, and we / upon thy name will call' (Psalm 80:18).

What are we really looking for at the Lord's Table? What are we really thirsting after? What do we really expect to receive? Well, it's feeding, strengthening, nourishing, refreshing that Christ gives to souls at his table, to those whom he loved with an everlasting love. That is what he bestows on them by his Holy Spirit from time to time, and that is what he especially intends to give them at his table. If we would be altogether dependent on him, we shall find that he is not slack in fulfilling his promise any more than he will be slack in fulfilling his judgment.

May he bless our meditation.

3 Repentance

O LORD, thou hast searched me, and known me. We are endeavouring on the basis of this verse to cover some of the subjects that call for self-examination in connection with the commemoration of the death of Christ. It is a requirement of God's Word, not only to examine ourselves whether we be of the faith, but to examine ourselves in connection with this ordinance: 'Let a man examine himself, and so let him eat of that bread, and drink of that cup.'

In order that we may examine ourselves rightly, we must desire and pray for and seek the guidance and teaching of the Lord himself, who alone knows us, as no other does. He knows us better than we know ourselves. He knows us immediately. He knows us through and through. He knows all that is true of us in the past and all that is true of us now, and of course all that shall be true of us in the future also. So we need to pray that the Lord would search us and know us, and that he would open up to us, in the light of his Word, what he finds in us.

The Lord delights to search and find what is in his people. Of course, he does find in them sins and wants. He does find in them many things that are contrary to his mind, by reason of the old nature that remains in them—and shall remain in them until they are made perfect in holiness at death. But he also finds in them the work of his own Spirit. The Spirit of God works in their souls in virtue of the death of the Redeemer, in virtue of the divine sacrifice of the Lamb of God outside the gates of Jerusalem. And when one considers the greatness of that sacrifice, then one can only expect that the fruits of such a great sacrifice will also be great in themselves. The sacrifice is great on account of the greatness of the person who died, the greatness of the price that was paid. The sacrifice is great also in the sense that it satisfied the claims of law and justice. Then, by reason and in virtue of the fulness of that sacrifice, the Holy Spirit begins the great work and the good work in the soul of a sinner, a great work which is precious in the sight of God and precious in the sight of God's people. This is what we are called on to examine ourselves in connection with: whether the root of the matter is in us.

What is the truth and measure of my repentance?

As we have already seen, the Lord's people are to examine themselves of various things—of their being in Christ, of their sins and wants, of the truth and measure of their knowledge and faith. And we now come to consider repentance, love to God and the brethren and so on, as we have it set out in the Larger Catechism.

As I mentioned already with regard to faith and knowledge, and must now stress once again with regard to repentance, the particular purpose of the examination which the soul is to conduct in the light of God's Word is first of all as to the truth or the reality of the possession of these graces in the soul, and then as to their measure, or the measure of their exercise. They are to examine the measure of knowledge, the measure of faith, and the measure of repentance. Why? Because where the root of the matter is, those who have grace *grow* in grace. Those who have spiritual life in their souls, who have the indwelling of the Spirit of God in the faculties of their souls, they grow in grace and in the knowledge of the Lord and Saviour Jesus Christ.

Examining growth in grace is like examining the growth in a flower. When you look at a flower in a garden, you do not see it visibly growing before you. Indeed, to all appearance there is no growth in the flower at all. The growth is only seen by looking back and comparing what it was once with what it is now.

This is how the growth of grace is to be examined in the soul. We do not see it grow by a direct look, and we do not appear to see it growing while we are looking. But when we compare grace as it is today with grace as it was before, we ought to be able to see growth, just as we would with a flower.

The grace of repentance is one of the outstanding graces of the Holy Spirit. It is a grace wrought by the Spirit of God in regeneration, in the quickening to spiritual life of the soul that is dead in trespasses and in sin. When the soul is regenerated, all the graces are now in the soul because of the life that is in the soul. The graces are but exercises of that new spiritual life. And this grace, the grace of repentance, is an exercise of the spiritual life that the Holy Spirit has put in the souls of God's people.

Therefore, you cannot have repentance—that is, saving repentance, repentance unto life—apart from the Spirit of grace and of supplications. You cannot have this grace of repentance apart from the saving work of God the Holy Ghost. You may have—and many do have—strivings which bring about 'legal repentance', that is, fear and dread of judgment, fear of death and fear of illness, fear of the hand of God and a consciousness of having offended God. But one may have that and still be in a state of nature. The grace of repentance is something that does not come from nature. It is spiritual. It comes from the operation of the Spirit of God. Where the Spirit of God is not, this grace is not, and where the Spirit of God is, the grace of repentance is.

Repentance involves a change of mind

The first thing to mention with regard to the grace of repentance is that repentance involves a change of mind. Repentance means a change of disposition, a change of mind and outlook. That is the fundamental meaning of repentance. That is why many of the older divines, Calvin among them, very often refer to repentance in the same terms as regeneration. They include the whole of regeneration or effectual calling under the term repentance, undoubtedly because of this view of repentance, that it is a thorough change of mind.

Now the question may be asked, and it is one that often exercises my own mind: 'How are we to make a distinction between faith and repentance?' That is, how are we to make a distinction in the exercise of the soul with regard to faith and repentance?

As we know, faith is the first exercise of the soul that is born again. By faith the born-again soul embraces and understands in some measure his own sinnership, his helplessness, and his need of salvation, and looks to the divine Redeemer for salvation. Then repentance comes in, as the result of faith. We can see this in the words in Zechariah, 'they shall look upon him whom they pierced'—that is faith—'and they shall mourn for him'—that is repentance.

Therefore, while faith and repentance are both in the soul at the time of regeneration—as indeed are all the graces of the Spirit—yet in order of logic, faith goes before repentance.

Nevertheless, it remains a question how to distinguish between faith and repentance. For instance, the prodigal son is an instance of repentance. You find him saying, 'I will arise and go to my father, and will say unto him,

Father, I have sinned against heaven, and before thee and am no more worthy to be called thy son: make me as one of thy hired servants.' That's the exercise of the grace of repentance—it was a returning to God, it was a coming to God. Now consider that on the one hand, and consider on the other hand that faith is also a coming. Repentance is a coming to God and faith is a coming as well, and therefore how are we going to distinguish between these two graces in their exercise in the spiritual experience of God's people?

I think we find the answer in the Word of God itself when the apostle speaks these words, 'repentance toward God, and faith toward our Lord Jesus Christ'. Faith, in coming to Christ for the pardon of sin and iniquity, has Christ as its particular object, and repentance, in returning to God, has God in Christ as its particular object.

If I may just digress for a moment, there are some words in Greek that take their meaning from the gospel, or they take their particular shade of meaning from the gospel. One of the mistakes often made in interpretation—and certainly indulged in by modern scholars—is to find out the meaning of the word as used by the Greeks, and to transpose that meaning into the Scriptures. However, there are words which have their particular shade of meaning from the very fact that they are used in a partic-ular way in the gospel itself.

If we allow for the moment that the root meaning of this Greek word for 'repentance' is 'change of mind', and if we grasp the fact that the particular object of repentance is God, and that the soul in repenting is returning to God and returning to God in Christ, then we reach this position with regard to repentance, that first of all it is a change of mind towards God.

But we must also grasp this particular shade of meaning, that repentance is a change of mind towards God with respect to my sins. That's why you find the Shorter Catechism saying, 'Repentance unto life is a saving grace, whereby a sinner, *out of a true sense of his sin* and apprehension of the mercy of God in Christ, doth, with grief and hatred of his sin, turn from it unto God, with full purpose of, and endeavour after, new obedience.'

That 'true sense of his sin' is something that the sinner has as a weighty burden. As David said, and as we were singing, it was such a burden that he could not lift up his eyes (Psalm 40:12). It was such a burden that it caused the publican in the temple to smite upon his bosom. He could not as much as lift up his eyes to heaven (Luke 18:13). This sense of sin is a weighty burden to the soul because he has had a change of mind with respect to God and with respect to his sins in the presence of God. As David said, 'My sin I ever see. / 'Gainst thee, thee only have I sinned / in thy sight done this ill' (Psalm 51:3-4).

By the light of God's Word, by the instruction of the Spirit of God, the sinner's sins are brought home to his soul and his conscience. He no longer sees these sins as he saw them before. Previously perhaps he regretted that he did them, and planned that some day he would repent of them. Or perhaps sin did not give him any concern at all, it did not appear to him to be of any consequence at all, and consequently he could live in sin without any regrets or any feelings of conscience. But now, as Paul says, 'the commandment came.' Sin had a spiritual resurrection in his soul, and he saw that he was worthy of death because of his sins against God.

Now the sinner sees these sins not merely to be a danger to himself, but to be against God. 'Against thee, thee only, have I sinned, / in thy sight done this ill' (Psalm 51:4). He sees these sins as sins that are abominable, sins that are worthy of death, and sins that have exposed him not only to the miseries of this life but to death itself and to the pains of hell for ever. He sees this, he understands it, because of a change in his heart and mind, so that he is no longer disposed to cover his sins, but his desire is to acknowledge them. 'I will confess my transgression,' David said. This spirit and mind is in him—to confess and to forsake these sins.

Leading up to repentance there may be much conviction of sin, of one kind or another. The sinner feels that his sins have placed him in a dangerous position—they have made him a child of wrath, and in themselves these sins will bring him lower than the grave. So he desires to be delivered from them for that reason. But also, you see, with regard to this change of mind that I am speaking of and this sense of sin that I am speaking of, secretly there's a regard—the sinner would not say love at this time, although it is the dawning of love—there is a regard and a care for the God against whom he has sinned. There's a secret longing and liking in the soul for God and an ashamedness on account of the fact that he has sinned against his God and he has transgressed his law. Secretly in the heart and mind of the sinner there is a movement of his heart and mind towards holiness that makes him feel that his sins are an abomination.

Repentance is towards God in Christ

Now, it's important for us to remember not just that repentance is towards God, but that it's specifically towards God in Christ. This true sense of sin that the sinner has makes him abhor himself. It makes him abhor that he has been what he has been—and especially, I may say, to abhor that he is what he is. He abhors that he finds in himself that which is completely contrary to God. This is what makes him feel so unclean. This is what made David say, 'O Lord, all that I do desire / is still before thine eye; / and of my heart the secret groans / not hidden are from thee' (Psalm 38:9). But repentance is towards God in Christ. It not only includes a true sense of sin, but it also includes what the catechism calls 'an apprehension of the mercy of God in Christ'. We cannot improve on the catechism definition of repentance.

As a true sense of sin gives him to abhor himself in God's sight, and makes him say, 'I have heard of thee by the hearing of the ear, but now mine eye seeth thee. Wherefore I abhor myself, and repent in dust and ashes' (Job 42:5–6), so this ray of spiritual light shining in from the sun of righteousness now rises with healing in the wings to his soul, so that he gets an apprehension of the mercy of God in Christ. It is like the first rays of the sun rising over the horizon. This can be seen in a very remarkable way in some tropical zones, such as the South Atlantic, where the sea is so flat that you can actually see the rim of the horizon. Before you see the sun at all, you begin to see these rays of the sun beginning to break the darkness of the night. So it is in connection with repentance. This apprehension of the mercy of God in Christ strikes in upon the soul. 'The Lord our God is merciful, / and he is gracious' (Psalm 130:8).

The soul gets a view of the mercy of God in *Christ*—this one through whom the mercy of God comes, the Son of God's love, the brightness of the Father's glory, the Prince of Peace, the Son of God who became the Son of man, whose body was broken and whose blood was shed for the remission of the sins of many. The soul looks on Christ and sees in him God's provision, and the provision of God's love, for a guilty, hell-deserving sinner such as he finds himself to be. He sees that in Christ there is a free pardon, in Christ there is mercy that is from everlasting to everlasting, in Christ there is peace for a sinner such as he finds himself to be. And this is provided by the love of God. It is provided by the love of the Father, and provided in the love of the Son, and now made known to the soul in the love of God the Holy Ghost.

When the sinner looks on Christ he sees the one who said, on account of the burden of sin which he bore, that the Father had brought him to the dust of death. Ah, my dear friend, it's the sinner who knows the burden of sin, and who knows the darkness of a true sense of sin, and his inability to deliver himself, that can get some understanding and some entrance into Jesus of Nazareth bearing the weight of the burden of his people's sins and addressing his Father and saying, 'Thou hast brought me'—with this burden—'to the dust of death' (Psalm 22:15).

And when he sees this, how abominable this sinner feels! What an awful thing sin appears to the soul who looks on Christ, the one who was pierced for the iniquity of the sins of many! How awful it appears to the one who mourns for the Saviour as he gets a view of his sufferings, who mourns for him with this mourning that views and understands in some measure what it cost the Son of God to redeem one sinner from his sins and to redeem his church by the shedding of his own precious blood! When the sinner sees what sin cost the Son of God, how abominable does sin appear! As his soul sees and views and tastes in some measure the mercy of God in Christ, what a sense of self-abhorrence he feels! He says like Jacob, 'I am not worthy of all the mercies and of all the truth which thou hast bestowed upon thy servant.'

Repentance is godly sorrow for sin. Repentance mourns over what sin caused the King of Zion to endure, what sin caused the High Priest to endure when he paid the great ransom price, when he laid down his life for the ungodly, and when he poured out his soul in his sufferings unto death, to make an end of sin and to bring in an everlasting righteousness.

Think of a sinner who sees the crown of thorns, who sees the nailed hands and the nailed feet and the pierced side, who hears the cry coming from the divine Saviour's broken heart, 'My God, my God, why hast thou forsaken me?' and who realises that this was all for the remission of the sins of many. My dear friend, don't you think that such a sinner cannot but mourn over what happened to that glorious one? Don't you think that he cannot but hate the sins—and these his own sins—that brought this glorious one to the cross and into the depths of these sufferings?

Ah, my dear friend, it is the apprehension of the mercy of God in Christ that brings the real sorrow for sin. This is what divorces the soul from his sins and makes him give his sins a bill of divorcement. If he had his own way he would never sin again against a God so merciful, against a God so gracious, and against a God of such infinite love, who gave his Son, the Son of his love, to pay this ransom price.

Repentance and new obedience

So, we have seen that repentance is towards God, and it's towards God in Christ, and it's towards the mercy of God in Christ. We have also seen that in repentance the sinner is brought to mourn over his sin, and to hate and to abhor it, and with grief and hatred to turn from it. This is his mind and this is his heart. As far as his will is concerned, he is done with sin. He desires to be done with sin. If he had his own way, as he gets these soul-refreshing views of Christ in the everlasting gospel and Christ on the cross of Calvary, he would desire not to sin ever again. He gives a bill of divorcement (as far as his will is concerned) to his sins and he desires to be free from them.

As the sinner turns from his sins with grief and hatred, he also has a resolution. He has a full purpose of and endeavour after new obedience. The prodigal son had this resolution. 'I will arise and go to my father.' 'I will be done with the far country, I will be done with the place of riotous living, I'll be done with satisfying the lust of the flesh and the lust of the eye and the pride of life. Instead I will turn my face toward God, and I'll turn my face towards God in Christ. This is the way that I desire to be going—to be returning to God all the days of my life. I desire to be among those who are returning to Zion.' 'The ransomed of the Lord shall return to Zion.'

My dear friend, the whole life of grace, from the moment of regeneration, is a life of returning to God, returning to Zion. Although they'll have sorrow and sighing on the way, nevertheless the Word says that the ransomed of the Lord shall return to Zion with songs and everlasting joy upon their heads, and sorrow and sighing shall flee away.

This is what we are called to examine ourselves on. Do we know a little about this repentance? This evangelical repentance, as it is called—gospel repentance, repentance unto life? This godly sorrow for sin that worketh repentance unto life that will not be repented of? The sorrow of this world worketh death. The sorrow of the natural man worketh death. The natural man may be sorry about his sins for a time, but it doesn't last. You may be here, for all I know, and when you go out of the church, you'll be saying to yourself, 'Well, from now on, I'll never go to any of these things that are condemned by the Word of God again.' Maybe that's what you said the last time you came out of a service. But what happened? You were sinning again in just the same way by Tuesday, Wednesday, Thursday! And why? Because you didn't repent! You were sorry and, under the common operations of the Spirit of God, as you were listening to the Word of God you had this desire to part with your sins and to part with your evil ways, and you were sorry, but it worked death. It never went any further.

But, you see, my dear friend, once you get to Christ, and to the mercy of God in Christ, and once you come to really have a soul appreciation and soul understanding of the death of Emmanuel in our nature, then you see sin in a different light. You cannot have sin *and* Christ on the throne of your heart. They cannot both be there at the same time. In repentance there is a coming to God, the eye of the soul is towards God in Christ, the soul has grief and hatred for his sin, and the soul has full purpose of and endeavour after new obedience.

Repentance is lifelong

Repentance is a grace which needs to be exercised as long as we are in this world. As I've been endeavouring to point out on other occasions, the life that is in the soul is exercised by way of faith, because we are still in this world. The reason for this is because we haven't reached heaven, because we are still journeying. We have faith in the promise and we are waiting for the promise to be fulfilled. The circumstances in which the soul is in this world require that he will be living by faith. 'Now abideth faith, hope and charity.' Faith and hope must be in exercise as long as the soul is in the world, because he's journeying to the land that the Lord has promised him, the heavenly country, and because he has not yet arrived, he must live by faith. He must live by faith in the promise, faith in the faithfulness of God, faith in the mercy of God, faith in the promise of God. As he lives that life, the life in his soul is exercised by way of faith.

The same is true with regard to repentance. As long as God's people are in this world they are sinners. Paul said, 'Christ Jesus came into the world to save sinners, of whom I am chief.' He did not say, 'I *was* chief.' He says in another place, 'I was a blasphemer, I was injurious,' but now he says, and he continued to say, 'I *am* chief.' Paul the aged, Paul the apostle, Paul the preacher of the everlasting gospel, Paul who was in the third heavens, who is he? He's Paul the chief of sinners! That's who you are too. You're a sinner, and you'll be a sinner all your days in this world, although at the same time you're an heir of heaven. The very fact that you feel yourself to be a sinner is a sign that you're an heir of God and a joint heir with Christ.

This illustrates the principle that repentance will always be needed in the soul in this world. You cannot get away from it, nor do I believe do you desire to get away from it, because you cannot get away from sin. Because you sin, therefore you need repentance. Because you sin, therefore you need a true sense of sin, and a soul-refreshing view of Christ in the everlasting gospel. That's what you need and that is what you're looking for. When you get that in your soul and when you are melted down with that in your heart and mind, how sweet the tears of repentance are, and how sweet is the abhorrence of sin that you feel in your soul!

Repentance comes after regeneration

Now the last thing I would like to notice is that repentance is an exercise of the regenerate soul. I must press this, perhaps not so much for the sake of God's people but for the sake of others who are here. Let us be quite clear on this point, my dear friend, that the repentance I am speaking about is the repentance of a regenerate soul, a soul that is born again.

I think it is very necessary to stress these points, or make these distinctions, because after all they are distinctions in the Word of God, and distinctions in the spiritual experience of God's people.

Before the sinner is born again there is such a thing as his being convinced of sin, his mourning over sin, his confessing his sins to God and his desiring to flee from his sins to Christ in the everlasting gospel. This is the case of the sinner who has come under concern of soul. Now, you must repent! The gospel says, 'Except ye repent, ye shall all likewise perish.' But very often Satan says to the soul, 'Now, before you come to Christ, you wait until you get proper repentance. You wait till you get properly satisfied about your repentance, and when you can weep and pray for a whole night, and when you can do this and that and the next thing, then you can come to Christ.'

But who's saying that to the soul? Satan! It sounds very pious, but it's Satan who's saying that to the soul. My dear friend, what Scripture calls on the sinner to do is to come to Christ. 'Now is the accepted time, and now is the day of salvation.' The gospel calls sinners to come to Christ, and you're to come to Christ *for repentance.*

It's part of the blindness and the darkness and the ignorance of man, as he is by nature, that he wants to weave repentance out of the belly of his own soul, and then he'll come to Christ and say, 'Lord, I've repented, pardon my sin.' Is Christ for a penitent sinner? Is he? Does Christ require, before he will receive a sinner, that he should be truly penitent? If that's so, then why does the Scripture say that Christ is exalted a prince and a saviour? For what? To *give* repentance unto Israel and the remission of sin.

If you wait, and if you heed the voice that says to you, 'Wait till you have proper repentance and wait till you're truly penitent, because Christ only will receive you when you're truly penitent,' you take care, my dear friend, because you'll never get to that stage—never, though you lived to the age of Methuselah. This cannot be too often stressed. Christ is for those who cannot repent. Christ is for those who cannot believe. That's the Christ of the everlasting gospel. Christ is for those who can do nothing for themselves. If you can do nothing, and you can't believe, and you can't repent, and you can't make yourself better, then I'll tell you this, my dear friend, you're the sinner that Christ is altogether suitable for. Even if you do not understand it now, the day will come, if that is your case, when you will understand that Christ is altogether suitable for you. You are to come to him for repentance.

Am I growing in repentance?

We need to examine ourselves about repentance—about our sins, about our mourning over our sins, about our confessing them, about our need of being divorced from them.

At the same time, we need to examine ourselves about our need of a faith's view of the Son of God's love, in order that we might genuinely repent, and in order that we might understand in a living way what Christ said, 'Take, eat: this is my body, which is broken for you.' Is not faith's view of Christ enough to melt down the sinner whose sins confront him and whose sins have come up around his head, whose sins are a weighty burden too great to be borne? Is it not enough to get a view in the Word of God of Christ as the one who died and rose again, or to get a view of Christ as the one who says, 'This is my body, which was broken for you'? Therefore, in connection with the continual exercise of repentance in the soul, there is a continual need for getting faith's view of Christ. There is a continual need for praying for Christ to make himself known to the soul. As the disciples said, 'How shalt thou make thyself known to us in another way than thou dost unto the world?'

This is what we need. We need it not only in connection with a communion season, but we do need it especially in connection with a communion season, so that we would grow in the knowledge of Christ as the one who died and bore the sins of his own people in his own body on the tree. At all times, and especially in view of the Lord's Supper, we need to look upon him whom we pierced— so that we would know this godly sorrow for sin, so that we would be melted down in our spiritual experience under the love of Christ as dying for the transgression of the sins of many, and so that we would come to the frame of mind that the church came to when she said, 'He was wounded for our transgressions, he was bruised for our iniquities: and the chastisement of our peace was upon him.'

If we are to have continued repentance, if we are to have what some of the older writers called the 'habit' of repentance, we must examine ourselves. According to the older writers, the 'principle' was introduced in regeneration; the 'habit' is exercised in the continued life of the child of God in this world. If we are to have the habit of repentance, then we must examine ourselves. Especially now when confronted with the Lord's Table, we are called on to examine ourselves as to the truth and measure of our repentance—the reality of our repentance and whether we are growing in repentance. Do we have exercises in our heart and mind where we're coming to God in Christ with a grief and hatred for sin, and where we're seeking a full purpose of and endeavour after new obedience?

You remember how it was in days gone by—you know it very well in your own experience. Did not the apostle remind the Galatians of how they had repented in days gone by, with what vehemence, and with what zeal they had cleared themselves of their sins and their iniquities? And is there not something similar, my dear friend, in your experience and mine? We knew what it was in days gone by to have renewed repentance towards God, a repentance that was renewed time and time again.

If we got something of that, my dear friend, it would be a great preparation for you and for me for sitting at the Lord's Table. Even if we didn't get it before the time, yet if we got it in the commemoration of the death of Christ, it would be a memorable occasion in time, and in eternity we will not forget it. May you and I be seeking this with our whole heart and mind.

May he bless his Word.